3 Sides to a Story

A family memoir about abuse, addiction, and admiration.

Debra Dillon
April Dillon
Krystal Dillon

Copyright © 2020 by Debra Dillon, April Dillon, & Krystal Dillon

All rights reserved.

ISBN:
Softcover 978-1-7357962-0-8

EBook 978-1-7357962-1-5

Table of Contents

Foreword	5
April's Side of the Story	6
Krystal's Side of the Story	13
Debra's Side of the Story	27
About the Authors	62

Foreword

Addiction is the villain that has broken up so many homes across the country. Not only does it affect the person with the disease, but it affects everyone that wants the best for them. We often find ourselves on an emotional rollercoaster over the self-destructive behavior of a family member. We convince ourselves that if they are happy with their bad decisions, then so are we. That false sense of contentment only lasts for so long before you find yourself drowning in "Whys" and "What Ifs" again. But have you ever taken a second to consider the fact that maybe you're the one being inconsiderate? Do you know what has caused your family member to choose the wrong path or if they even had a choice? "3 Sides to a Story" allows you to understand the circumstance from every angle.

-Deborah Collins, Author

April's Side of the Story

I wasn't sure if I was tired of it, or if I was just scared, but I needed an escape from my mom's world. Growing up with my mother ended at the age of 10 for me. That's when I decided to live with my grandmother. My mom was always like a sister to me. I can't recall her ever chastising me, or my sister, Krystal, for that matter. My mom was fun. She was beautiful and everyone loved to be around her. She always kept a nice place to stay and a nice car. I used to love to sit in the back seat of her drop-top mustang, with my hair hitting my face from the wind blowing. The singer Prince would be blasting out of the speakers as we rode through the city of Hammond. Our home was right next door to my grandmother's house, which worked out great for me. I enjoyed the best of both worlds.

The party was always at our spot. My mom had a black leather sofa and these huge white decorative cats in the living room. Mirrors were everywhere because she liked to look in them while she danced. We had the best speaker system too. I remember my grandmother calling over to our house, saying, "Turn that damn music down!" All we had to do was tell my mom what we wanted and we had it. The best times were staying up all night with my little cousins. They were like brothers and sisters to us. We loved to eat this meal that she made out of fried cornbread. She would tell us stories and sing to us.

I couldn't help but notice the change in my mother's behavior early on. Her drug addiction became evident. She started to sleep in later and later. She started to fight her peers. She stopped showing my sister and I attention. One night, she drove to this lady's house with my sister and I in the car. There were so many people outside screaming and shouting, "Kick that bitch ass!" I remember telling my little sister not to look. I couldn't believe my mom was fighting. There was either a fight or a party when I was with my mother from that moment going forward.

Because of her actions, I permanently moved in with my grandmother. I felt embarrassed and more importantly, heartbroken all the time. My little sister stayed with my mom up until her arrest, about a year or so later. This is when my grandmother asked my mother to sign over her parental rights. My grandmother and aunt did the best that they could, picking up the pieces that my mother left behind. My grandmother made our clothes and my aunt did our hair. They became our mother figures. My grandmother is my rock and has taught me everything in life.

My mom's sister and I are very close to this day. She had one son, so taking care of two girls back then was a challenge for her. She continued to do an amazing job. I remember at 13 years old, getting my first period. My grandmother and aunt made such a big deal about it. We had cake and ice cream. My aunt did my hair and we went shopping. All I could think about was my mom's absence at such an important time in my life.

How could she let drugs take her away from us? I just thank God that my grandmother was able to step up and take my sister and I in. Many of my peers that were in similar situations weren't so lucky. I only had a small group of friends that I knew I could trust with concealing the fact that I had a mother that was addicted to crack cocaine. I would never invite my friends over out of fear that at any moment my mother would return home from the streets and be outside asleep in an old, abandoned car, or on the carport until my grandmother felt sorry enough to allow her to come inside.

I also tried to kill myself at the age of 13. I remember it like it was yesterday. I swallowed a bottle of pills. I didn't know what they were. I just wanted them to put me to sleep and out of my misery. I was sitting outside talking to God while I waited. I hoped this would bring my mom home so that she could take care of my little sister. My cousin saw me sitting there pitiful and said, "Nikki, get up. You will be alright". I remember that vividly. Even though I thought I had reached a point of accepting the situation, my sister never healed from my mom's choice of choosing drugs over us. I wanted my sister to be happy.

My mother wasn't in jail very long, but it was still enough time for her to lose everything. She had no house, no car, or a job. She would continue to go from house to house, rehab to rehab, and man to man. I learned at a young age that crying and begging for someone to stay with you doesn't work. I would cry until my head would hurt. I would beg my mother to stay, but she never did. My grandmother, my aunt, and my sister were there for every birthday, band recital, and graduation. I can even recall my father attending my high school graduation. My mother came around shortly after, seeking money and pain pills.

I needed my mother. Oh, how badly did I need my mother. We tried over and over again to get her help. It never lasted, so I stopped getting my hopes up. I started to expect disappointment before it happened. I would cope with it by eating food. I think my grandmother and I both did. This was the way that many people in my community dealt with issues: drugs, church, or food. Overall, my grandmother did the best that she could with what she had. I am forever grateful for that.

Coming of age, dating was nonexistent for me. I never really wanted a boyfriend, but I was "friendly". I liked to have parties and be on the go with my friends. My grandmother taught us that once you let someone in, they would hurt you. She was basing that off of her past experiences. Therefore, I avoided love as long as I could. It's not that I didn't want a connection, I was afraid of one.

At the age of 23, I decided to try something new. I wanted to try love, but I didn't quite know how. I was possessive, eager to please, and always craving intimacy. I wanted everyone around me to be happy at all times. I wanted things to be perfect. That same year, I got my first real boyfriend. I became pregnant but the relationship didn't last. Here I was, pregnant, alone, and afraid. After my first trimester, I found out that my son would be born with potter syndrome, which meant that my child would be born without kidneys. I carried my son full-term. I wanted to watch him take his last breath in my arms.

That was a heartache that I can't explain. My mom still wasn't there. I eventually went on to have 4 more beautiful children. My mother made it towards the end of each pregnancy. Her intentions were good, I told myself. I knew she wanted to be there for me, but her addiction would have her around me only for the medication I was given for pain.

Just recently, my mom was home for 3 months. The entire family was happy. She was spending so much time with me and my children. I looked at her and told her that I loved having her around. The next day she was gone. I cried a little and moved on. I'm used to it now. My mom is in her 60's. My sister and I are grown, in our 30's. Last week, she was working, this week she's back on the streets, sleeping in cars. My children miss their grandmother just as badly as I miss her.

The way my mother raised us made me want to be a better mother. I will never allow anything or anyone to stop my love or support for my kids. She always kept a man around me and my little sister, and we would always end up calling them "dad". I knew I wanted something different. For the first time in my life, I'm happy. To say that I'm happy is a huge step forward for me. Happiness scares me, but I can no longer live in fear.

Krystal's Side of the Story

My mom and I would ride through Hammond, Louisiana a lot. I'd always have a happy meal, some Reese's and a bag of Doritos chips. She would leave me in the car sometimes. I'd fall asleep while she would run into her friends' house for "her medicine". One day I got scared because a strange man kept walking past the car. I got out to knock on the door of the house just to find my mom inside, looking frightened. She was hiding behind a washing machine in a little room that was on the side of the house. I later found out that she was hallucinating because she had just smoked crack cocaine. There were several other times this happened after that particular incident. Another night, I stayed with my mom in her apartment and she woke me out of my sleep. She was freaking out, asking me to hang stuff in the windows because there were people trying to get in. This was the last time I wanted to stay with her at my own will because it scared me so badly.

"Momma, please! Please, don't leave me!" I cried out. I remembered my grandmother standing over me, waking me from the nightmare that I was having of my mom walking away from me. I was only 8 years old when I had that dream but it still haunts me today. I've always wanted to be under my mother. I remember the smell of Doral cigarettes and her Sand & Sable perfume that seemed to linger around even after she was long gone. My grandmother and my mom would always fight over me and my sister's things. Even though I wanted to follow my mom, my older sister never wanted to go. My mom would pack up all of our clothes, even the food she bought, and we'd leave my grandmother's house. We would walk to wherever someone would allow us to stay. We'd always end up back at my grandmother's house and mom would be gone again. I never understood why she didn't want me. I thought I was a good kid. I worked really hard in school thinking that my mother would be so proud of me that she would come home and want to stay home.

Growing up without my mother in my life was rough. It wasn't that my grandmother didn't provide for me, but I still longed for that mother-daughter bond. It wasn't like my father was in the picture either. He was also an addict, so his mom would help my grandmother with me. I remember the little gifts that my dad's mother would make me for the holidays. She would make me little tins filled with different types of cookies and goodies. In the meantime, my mom had me calling at least three different men "daddy" so that she could get money from them. As a child, I was so confused as to why anyone would do that. However, if it kept her around, I did it. Reflecting on the different men she would have around me when I was younger, one in particular stood out. We had a mobile home right next door to my grandmother's house. I was maybe 6 or 7 years old. I remembered being in the living room when he picked me up and sat me on his lap. I tried to get up but he just held me there. My mom walked in a few minutes later. I remember her screaming that he was holding her baby with his dick on hard. She started shooting at him and he left running out of the back door. There was another occasion when I was really young, that he tried to kidnap me. My great-grandmother stopped him with a meat cleaver. She made him take me back home. Our great-grandmother was the glue of the family. She always took my mom in and gave her money when she needed it. I see now that it only enabled her. Maybe if the family showed her tough love from the beginning, she would have gotten better.

Things eventually worsened. My mom began to stay gone for longer periods of time. I just knew one day something bad was going to happen to her out there. One cold, rainy day, I had forgotten my jacket at home. I still had to catch the school bus on time. The school secretary called home and told my grandmother that I was cold and without a jacket. My grandmother sent my mother to the school. I hadn't seen her in about two weeks. At that time, parents could just ask for your classroom number and walk to your class without the hassle of today's school entry regulations. They didn't have as much security as they do now. Here I am, in class, when I look up to see my mother wearing shorts that were so short you could see her underwear, a ripped black shirt, with fishbone earrings that were so big that they stretched her earlobes. Her hair was a complete mess as she walked towards my desk to hand me my jacket. I'd never felt so embarrassed. I just placed my head down and listened to the kids around me laugh and mock her. That was the moment that I felt the pain of embarrassment and it was because of my mother.

One day later in the school year, I was called to the front office. I was met by a short lady and a man waiting on me. They needed to speak with me about my mother. I immediately got emotional because I thought something bad happened. They assured me that she was fine, but they needed to know who took care of me. They took me into an empty office and started to ask questions about who cooks and feeds me and my sister. "Where do you sleep? Who all lives with you? Do you feel safe?" Were a few of the many questions they asked me. I didn't know what to think and answered every question as honestly as I could. Once I made it home, I told my grandmother what happened earlier that day at school. She just replied, "Good." She then walked off. It wasn't long before I found out that those people were OCS workers and that my mother had lost her parental rights over us. I think this caused my mother's addiction to get worse. A month or more had passed before I saw her again.

"Y'all momma is in the hospital." My grandma informed us one night, as she hung up the phone with someone. "What's wrong with momma?" I asked. I don't remember ever seeing my grandma cry before. Tears were running down her face. "Is she okay?" I continued to dig. "She's at Seventh Ward Hospital." My grandma replied. "I'm going to see now." She added on. When she came home from the hospital, grandma told us that our mom had gotten in the car with a guy that was a trick and he made her strip naked. He then told her he was going to kill her, so she jumped out of the car. She scarred herself up pretty badly. She had rocks embedded in her skin and blood was everywhere. She managed to get away and find help. I thanked God that the trick didn't kill my mom and that she was safe. Now she could come home and be a mother to us. Now, she would be afraid of returning to the streets. Unfortunately, it didn't last long. She went back to the streets after 3 months. My mom has been in and out of at least six rehab facilities that I can remember. I remember taking long rides with my grandmother and aunt to visit her on several different occasions. After each stay, she would end up back on the streets. The rides to rehabilitation centers became rides to different crack houses to look for her. We wanted to make sure she was still alive. That would at least ease my grandmother's mind. It became so routine that I started to pick up on the cycles of what she was doing and why. It was all for pity. She knew that as soon as it looked like she wanted to change, my grandmother would let her come home.

Over the years ahead, I put my focus into school. I just wanted to be somebody in life. Having a mother and father that were both drug addicts, who basically put their habits before their child, was heartbreaking enough. My mom eventually met this guy that she seemed to like a lot. He lived on Mooney Avenue in an old, white house. There were a bunch of jars in the kitchen and it always smelled like burned plastic. My cousin and I went to visit her one day, when my mother and her boyfriend got into a big fight. He put us out of his house and we had to walk from his house all the way back to my grandmother's house. It seemed to take forever. She ended up marrying that man. Their relationship was a rocky one. They were always fighting and shooting at one another. She even ran him over with a car.

In the meantime, my hard work was paying off. I finally graduated from high school. Graduating from high school was a great accomplishment for me. I graduated at the top of my class and wanted nothing more than my family to be proud of me. My mother and my father were both in attendance. I smile even now when I think about it. I went to a local university shortly after, but later decided to attend school in Monroe, Louisiana, with one of my cousins. My mom was doing better around this time and wanted to take me to my college orientation. I was so happy to have her involved in something that was a major life event for me. She rented us a hotel room and bought me my first drink. We partied and enjoyed ourselves. I'll never forget that. She appeared to be on the right path. Come to find out, the man she married was also her drug dealer and she was only around more because drugs were easier to get. By drugs being easier to obtain, her addiction worsened. I thanked God that my grandmother was there for my sister and I, because I'm not sure where we would be if she hadn't stepped up.

I didn't realize how much my childhood affected my own relationships. I ended up marrying the man of my dreams, and giving birth to three beautiful children. My husband became abusive. He also cheated, but I wanted the marriage to work so badly for my children's sake. I wanted them to experience a home with both the mother and father, but we ultimately divorced. I went through terrible depression after my divorce. I started drinking a lot and was going out to nightclubs almost every weekend. I was drinking to go to bed and to wake up in the mornings. No one really noticed. One day, I received a call from my aunt who lived in Michigan. She said that she had a dream about me drinking. She could actually name the types of alcoholic beverages that I would buy. I poured them all down the drain immediately and I prayed against the power of alcoholism.

Not long after getting my own life back on track, my father had come home from a rehab stay he was on for the past few years. He helped me more and we formed a bond. My father also formed a bond with my children. My kids finally had a pawpaw. I felt so much joy and excitement just from knowing that he cared enough to try to pick up the pieces. Being back in the area with old friends, his demons resurfaced. He was found dead shortly after, in a crack house in Amite City from an overdose. My heart crumbled, not just because he died, but because of the cause of death. I hoped that my mother would not meet this same fate.

As time passed, I started dating a younger guy that finally made me feel wanted and sexy. I was having so much fun that I overlooked the fact that I was being used and cheated on again. We had a daughter together who had some health complications. Fortunately, I gained some wonderful friends that helped me with her along the way. I made unhealthy attachments to people because of the abandonment of my parents. I would have high expectations for people that could not live up to them. I wanted to feel the same love and loyalty that I was giving to others. I had my days of thinking I was living in a curse from my parents' bad decisions in their own lives. I wanted to be a good, successful mother. I started to put so much energy into my children, that I would sometimes neglect myself. I was also afraid to be alone, causing me to stay in situations that were not good for me. My eagerness for my children to experience a two parent home was not only hurting me, but them as well.

Growing up without a mother or a father's touch can take its toll on a person. Until you have children of your own, you'll never completely understand the effects of neglect. You can only pray that you are nothing like your parents. I've grown to be so overprotective of my own children. I once had a very heated argument with my mom about my oldest daughter. Whenever my mom would start doing well, my sister and I would let her keep her grandkids from time to time. One day she kept my oldest daughter for me. My daughter, who was only 4 years old at the time, answered my mom's cell phone when I called to check on her. I asked her where her grandmother was and she replied, "In her friends' house getting her medicine." I asked my daughter where her grandmother was again, but she just kept stating that she was sitting in the car waiting on Maw Maw. I immediately got so angry and afraid all at the same time. I recollected sitting in the car for hours waiting on my mother for that same reason she gave my daughter. Once I was able to speak with my mother about bringing my daughter back to me, I said some very hurtful things to her. Under the influence, she responded by stating that she should have never had me.

I've been calling my mom by her first name since I was about 10 years old. I would get in trouble for calling her "mom" by my grandmother, who was our legal guardian at the time. I felt more like my mother's sister than her daughter. I honestly think I've done more for her than she has done for me. There have been times that I have been so embarrassed because of the things she does and it breaks my heart to hear people refer to her as a crackhead. She seems to get a rise out of the attention. She has told us about her many near-death experiences and how she would trick for money.

I've watched a lot of documentaries about addiction and how it attacks the mind. Why is it so hard for my mother to shake this? Why do we have to watch her kill herself? Does she not have enough remorse or love for her daughters to just try? As painful as this is for me, I've begun to tell myself that this is the way she wants to live her life. It honestly makes me angry. I wish with every breath in me that I could just go on and pretend like she doesn't exist, but I can't. I know my mother can heal from this but the question is does she want to?

I know she has a good heart, but I can't help but to hate that she chose to travel down such a horrible road in life. She told us stories about how she got addicted to drugs and how the people that introduced her to them are now clean and living good lives. Why did my mom have to remain this way? It hurts never knowing when we will get another call saying something bad has happened to her. My sister and I speak about it all of the time. I wonder how we would feel. Will we mourn or be happy that she is finally at rest and off of the streets? We may not have the perfect history, but my mother and I are both strong women in our own right. I can only pray that she decides a better direction for her life to go in. Either way, she has children and grandchildren that love her.

Debra's Side of the Story

I don't remember too much about my childhood for some reason. I block a lot out, maybe because it was painful, or maybe I just simply don't remember. In the 60's we didn't have much to remember. Born in Hammond, Louisiana in 1962, I am 1 of 5 children. My mother said she always wanted a little black girl that looked just like her, and I look just like my mom. I was always active and moving around. At the age of 2, my mom recalls feeding me on the kitchen floor. All of a sudden, I passed out cold. She remembers screaming and shaking me. She would act it out, saying, "Baby, wake up! Baby, wake up!" I would become warm inside, as if I could remember, or wanted to, at least. My mother picked me up and ran down the road with me in her arms, trying to find someone to bring us to the hospital. As she arrived on my aunt's doorstep, she said I took a deep breath and looked up at her smiling, like nothing ever happened. She took me to the hospital anyway. The doctor informed her that all the running and shaking she did must have loosened whatever was down in my windpipe. My mother knew then that I was a blessed child.

At the age of 5, I remember my parents having to raise money for our church. What we did in the old days was something called a king and queen pageant. I was so happy that it was my turn to be in the church pageant and represent our family! I couldn't believe that I won. I felt like a true queen when they put that crown on my head. I felt so beautiful. The next year it was over and another little girl became the new queen. I didn't feel pretty anymore. I felt so ugly, inside and out. Who needs pageants anyway? After that, I became a tomboy! I would hang with the boys in the woods all day. I would leave my one sister at home to play with my other cousins. I could fight too! If anyone said anything to me, or anyone in my family, I would fight! I fought boys and girls. It felt good to be the one my family looked up to.

I remember my mother and my grandmother going to town. They would always leave us kids with our grandfather. He would call us inside one by one. We were always afraid of him because he carried a big gun around all the time. When I would go inside, he would make me lay on the bed. He would kiss me on my lips. I can still taste the tobacco he would chew in his mouth. He would rub on my vagina and would make me rub on his penis until it would stand straight up. One day he laid on top of me. I asked, "Papa, what are you doing?" I had tears running down my face. He told me if I ever told anyone about this, then he would kill me. I was very afraid of him. My mother was doing the laundry one day and called me in to ask why my panties were stuck together. She wanted to know what I had been doing. I told her it was because my seat came off of my bike and I slipped.

I recall having a good mother. She was always there for us. We would wake up in the morning to a big pan of biscuits on the table. She cried a lot. I think it was because my father did not come home most nights. My father was hardly ever around. This made my mom sad and angry. I remembered when he did come home because it wasn't often. My father loved to gamble. He would jump on my mother and take back the money he gave her for our bills. My sister was so afraid that she would hide in the closet. She would put clothes on top of her head and my older brother would jump out of the bedroom window. My baby brother would just sit on his bed, but not me. I would be right by my mother's side, making sure that she was alright.

At the age of 10, I remembered living in the brick house that my mother and father built. My father had a big family with seventeen siblings. Three of his brothers came to live with us. One of my uncles who came to live with us would play with me all the time. He was like my best friend, in a way. My father and mother owned a nightclub, so my uncles were the babysitters. While lying in my bed one night, I got up to take a bath and my uncle raped me. I remembered the pain and me screaming, but he did not stop. I felt so ashamed. I thought it was my fault, since my mother would tell me that I was always too fast, hanging with the boys. I knew everyone would blame me, so I didn't tell. I had a free spirit and I was too friendly. That was my curse. As time went on, I continued to fight as a coping mechanism from the family trauma I had experienced.

One day, we had a family dinner at our house and I choked on a chicken bone. It was stuck in my throat and I couldn't breathe! My mom picked me up by my feet and shook me over and over, until I passed out. This was the second time this had happened. Once I woke up, I threw the chicken bone up. That was the last memory I had of living in the brick house before we lost it. My mom worked to make ends meet. My father continued to gamble all the money away. She did all she could to support us kids and my uncles. Soon, the uncle that raped me went back to live with my grandmother. I was glad he was gone.

We moved into a very small house. It had three rooms. My mother made those three rooms work. There were two bedrooms, a kitchen, and a bathroom. We had to haul our water. My mother had a big bucket for the toilet and we had to take one bath a week at my grandmother's house. We were happy there! Growing up, the kids would make fun of our home. I couldn't understand why they were making fun of our home. Hell, it was the cleanest house on our road. My father taught my brother how to keep up the lawn. That I can say he did. He did a pretty good job too. My mother put so much love into that little house.

Me and my oldest brother would fight all the time. One day, we had it out with a jar. He threw me behind the sofa, beating me in the head with the jar. He was the baddest of the bunch. My mother stayed on his ass. My middle brother was very quiet and to himself. He was always fixing things, like radios and other appliances. He would find things and take them apart, then put them back together. One day he was minding his own business, when our older brother was up to his usual, which was picking on people. My middle brother went and told my mother to make him leave him alone. My mother was busy in the kitchen, so she told him to pick up something and just hit him with it. My brother did just that. He picked up an axe and hit my oldest brother with it. My mom asked him why he got an axe and my brother replied, "You told me to pick up something and hit him with it." Mom said, "I didn't mean to kill him. I just wanted you to hit him. What is wrong with you kids!" I remembered us all laughing together that day. My oldest brother got away with a lot and my middle brother ran away a lot.

At the age of 16, we were allowed to go out. I had to be home before the party got started off good. I always wanted to leave home anyway, because I did not approve of my mother's boyfriends after she and my father parted ways. The first one we liked pretty well. He could build things. When he finished building my uncle and aunt's house right next to ours, he helped my mom add on to hers. They broke up. She met another man. My soon-to-be husband and I met while I was attending one of the parties they had thrown. Yes, I married my first husband at age 16. I was pregnant soon after, but I miscarried at 3 months. We moved into a small apartment. I was in the 10th grade going to the 11th grade, when I quit school. I don't know what the reason was, but I just quit.

My husband liked to drink a lot. I didn't drink or do drugs. One night, he came home drunk after being out with his brothers and wanted to have sex with me. My aunt was going to visit the next day, so I wanted the apartment to be nice and clean. I was tired from all of the cleaning. My husband attempted to carry me to the bed and I started swinging with a box cutter in my hand. His blood went everywhere. I ran next door. I heard him beating on the door behind me. His brother came back and heard him screaming. His brother informed him that he was losing a lot of blood and that he needed to go to the hospital. My friend drove me to my mom's house. My husband had 90 stitches inside and out. My mom was a nurse, so she nursed him back to health. I would cry at night because he was in so much pain. That boxcutter wasn't meant for him. It was for my grandfather and my uncle. We eventually broke up because I did not love him anymore.

As time went on, I had found the love of my life, or so I thought. He was my everything! I was very much in love with this man. He was the most beautiful, handsome man that I had ever seen. He wasn't from Louisiana, which made things even more exciting. My sister and I worked at a restaurant in downtown Hammond. Any time I was at work, he would ask me to bring him something to eat. I didn't mind because he was my man. I would arrive at his apartment with his food and make love to him over and over again. I got pregnant at the age of 21. Here I was, pregnant for a man that I loved so much. I don't know why, but the feeling he gave me was like no other. I was going to make him love me equally. My mom did not like him at all, so he stopped coming over to see me. I didn't understand why my mom would run off someone that loved me. He was the father of my child. I let her control my life and I was afraid to say anything. She would put me out of her house if I did. I did not see him for a long time. All I did was clean the house while my mom was at work, or sit in my room and listen to music.

My life became very boring. I had no friends. You couldn't come to my mom's house because she didn't like visitors. Sometimes, I would walk down the road to visit my grandma. We would sit and talk for a long time. My mom would go to the club with all of her friends after work. At this time, I was about 5 months pregnant. Mahogany's kicking felt like something I've never felt before. Mahogany was going to be my baby's name. The father of my child worked at their family-owned grocery store. He was one of the cashiers there. We'd go by there all the time after my doctor's visits. One day, he came over to my mom's house and brought me a bottle of red wine and a pickle. I told him the doctor informed me that I was anemic. I was so happy that my love was back in my life! He must've cared. Mahogany's father just knew I was in love with him. He had me right where he wanted me.

As the months passed, I had a beautiful baby girl. My baby was due on April 22nd, my mother's birthday. However, she did not arrive until May 2nd, 1981. Everyone was there for her birth. She was 8 lbs and 9 oz. She was my first little girl, so I wanted everything to be perfect. While in the hospital, I was telling my mom about the name, Mahogany, that I had chosen for my baby. She replied, "You're not going to name her that. She won't know how to spell that when she goes to school." My mom changed her name to April instead. I gave her the middle name Nicole. I hadn't gotten divorced yet, so my baby had to take the last name of my husband.

Once I returned home from the hospital, my brothers took my baby out of my arms. Here I was, still sitting in the car, waiting for them to come help me out of it. With all of those stitches I had inside of me, all I could remember was needing help to move around. No one came, so I helped myself. By the time I made it inside, everyone was laughing and looking at my baby, as if she was the prettiest thing they'd ever seen. April was way too big for me and tore my insides up pretty badly during birth. The doctor had me on a lot of pain medications because of that, so I took some and layed down. My mom quickly took over. She wouldn't even let me sleep with my own baby, saying things like, I might roll over on her. Of course, I believed her. My mom wanted the baby all the time, so it wasn't like I had to be alert. She would feed her and take her to all of her doctor's appointments. That left a lot of time on my hands.

I still pursued my child's father and continued to sleep with him. Time just flew by. April was becoming more beautiful each day. I would buy her clothes just because they were cute. I could remember one day, when she was about 2 years old, she was running around the house. Everybody was calling her name, saying, "Come to me! Come to me!" She would only come to me, her mom. April was so bad at times. I would put her in the tub to give her a bath and she would splash water all over me. I would laugh, saying, "You splashed water all over your mommy's clothes!" I would get in the tub with her. When we were done, I would dry her off and wrap the towel around her. When I would open the bathroom door, she would take off running with the towel. This one time, my mom said, "Come here, Debbie. Hurry up!" I replied, "I'm coming!" She wanted me to see how beautiful my daughter was. While she was standing in the doorway, I went to get the camera to take a picture of her. I have that picture still today.

Over time, my younger sister had gotten married. She hadn't had any kids yet, so she spent a lot of time with my child. She took her everywhere she went. My sister even took professional portraits with April. They are still on the wall today. She was the first person to take my child to the zoo. She was a great aunt. She was always a homebody, unlike myself. I liked going to the bar rooms. That's when I started drinking. I liked the feeling that drinking gave me. It made me feel free. I knew my baby was alright because she was in my mother or my sister's care. Once I got home to try to spend time with my child, all of Hell would break loose. It had to be mom's way or no way. She wanted to be in control, so basically, I had a child for my mom.

I eventually started to receive welfare and food stamps. I would pay my mom about fifty bucks a month to stay with her, and I would make groceries for the house. My mom had gotten another boyfriend that we called Mr. B for short. One day, April was playing on the floor when Mr. B came along and picked her up. He bounced her up and down. April laughed and giggled. While playing, April accidentally pulled down a mirror, clocking Mr. B right in the head. Blood was everywhere. Mr. B told my mom to come and get my baby, stating that she cut him. Mom replied to Mr. B, "You better not touch that girl. You shouldn't have been playing with her!" Mr. B then told my mom to whoop April or he was going to leave. Needless to say, we never saw Mr. B again.

I eventually got pregnant again. I was not ready for that, but I was going to keep my unborn child anyway. My brothers were so angry when they found out that I was pregnant again. When I was around 2 months pregnant, I lost the baby. That was the end of my baby's father as well. I started back going out to nightclubs and that is when I met a tall, dark glass of chocolate milk. We danced all night long. My family loved to be on the dance floor. I ended up leaving with "Mr. Chocolate Milk". He was a real man and did not ask me for sex the first night that he took me home. He took me to breakfast the next morning and we talked for a while. He told me where he worked and that he had his own mobile home. I was feeling that idea because I wanted to leave my mother's house badly.

He finally took me to his home. He had one of the nicest mothers I'd ever met. His father and one of his sisters lived in Hammond. His mother and his other sister lived in Amite City. Mr. Chocolate and I were the perfect couple until I moved in with him. That is when he started to abuse me. My baby was around 3 years old when she was doing what 3 year olds do- which was running, jumping and playing. This day she was in the bedroom, a little too quiet. I went to check on her. My baby had a strange needle in her hand. I wasn't sure if it was a diabetic needle or not, but it didn't matter to me. I called my mom and she told me to get her baby out of there quickly. She told me that I could stay there if I wanted to, but bring her baby back home to her. I didn't want to be without my child so I went back home as well.

I would still sneak and see Mr. Chocolate on the side so that my family would not judge me. I eventually ended up pregnant again. During this pregnancy, I was taking a lot of pain pills every day. The pain pills gave me energy. They replaced the pain and emptiness that I was feeling. I was taking Tylenol 3's. They were mild, so I did not think they would harm me or the baby. Besides, the doctor was the one prescribing them for me. One night, when I was around 8 months pregnant, Mr. Chocolate called me on the phone at 2 am in the morning. He said, "Baby, I'm sorry for calling you so late. Get up. I'm coming to pick you up." I got up and put some clothes on. By the time I was finished dressing, he was at the back door. We left and headed to his house. I was wondering why his friends were still in the car, but I did not say anything. I assumed they just wanted to ride with him. Once we got to his house, I saw a car in the yard. It belonged to a good friend of his. His friend was accompanied by his girlfriend. The couple was so high and drunk.

Mr. Chocolate showed them to the bedroom that my daughter used to sleep in. He said, "Baby, why are you sitting in the living room? You know where the bed is." I went into his room. I sat on his bed waiting for him to explain to me what was going on. He started to take my clothes off and I told him to stop. I asked him again what was going on. That's when he replied, angrily, "Don't play stupid with me! You know why you're here!" I said, "No." I walked out of the room. He followed me. He opened his back door and threw me outside. There was a big pine tree outside of his door. Of course when he threw me out, I hit the tree very hard. He then came out to pick me up. He slapped the shit out of me. By this time, I started screaming for his mom. She lived next door. She heard my screams and came running over to help me. She noticed the blood. She made him stop hitting me and she took me over to her house. I went to the bathroom and I saw a lot of blood. I asked her to bring me to the hospital, with tears running down my face. She told me that my baby and I would be alright. She said she would bring me home. I listened to her, being that she was a head nurse. She suggested that I go lay down. I did so, still bleeding as I lay there. I thought it was because she did not want me to get her son in trouble, that she would not take me to the hospital. I spent the rest of the morning at her house. Once we got in her car the next morning, I looked over at his house. His car was still there. I assumed he picked up another girl after the incident. I said to myself that it was the first and the last time he'd ever hit me. Once home, I got out of the car and I told his mother, "Thank you." She replied, "You're welcome. Y'all will be alright. He was just drunk."

Mr. Chocolate started seeing the woman he picked up after he jumped on me that night. He would hang up on me when I would call him. When he did decide to answer, he'd say things like, "Leave me alone. I have someone else." He said that we would cross that bridge once we got to it, referring to my pregnancy. Eventually, I gave birth to Krystal, which was not an easy delivery. Krystal would not turn in my belly. My auntie was with me the whole time, since my mom was at work and my sister was home taking care of April. The rest of the family were at the hospital. They kept saying how pretty Krystal was once she arrived. She had a lot of cold black hair. She looked just like her father.

I would put pillows around Krystal to prop her up next to me. I would then take three pain pills because I was in so much pain. I had done it many times before and I knew it wouldn't harm me. I can't begin to tell you how good they made me feel. I would take more pain pills any time that I started to hurt, but I was still able to function like a normal person . I would make milk bottles and make sure my children were fed. They were always dressed nicely, with their hair combed neatly. As time went on, I ran into an old friend that I used to date way back in the day. As the old saying goes, things happen. They also say if someone comes back, that means it was meant to be. I just called him My Baby. In the beginning, he was a very good guy. He had a good job so we rented my brother's mobile home, which was like new. About a month later, I got a job working at the state school helping disabled people. "This is it!" I thought to myself. My home was beautiful. I had everything a woman could ask for. I kept my girls looking good. My mom lived right next door so I had a babysitter whenever I needed one. When I had to go to work, I would still take pain pills. No one knew that I was buying pills from my friends.

My Baby hung out with one of my male cousins a lot. They went everywhere together. I'm not sure why they liked each other's company so much, but he and I were going steady together. We both were working at the time, so my daughters were spoiled to the point where they didn't wear the same pair of shoes twice. After a while, however, I started to miss work and he would too. We started to have fights. One day we got into a fight about a pork chop and I ended up shooting him in the foot. That's when my life started to go downhill. Life became blurry because of my abuse of pain pills. I couldn't get out of bed without the help of a pain pill. This was not the life that I was used to. I could not think for myself, or do anything else for that matter. My mom had to step in and do my motherly duties, such as dressing my girls, cooking their food, and cleaning my house. She also took them to their doctor's appointments. She really saved the day.

I tried everything to get off of pain pills, so I thought. I will never forget this particular

Monday, when My Baby and my cousin were hanging out, per usual. They were riding in my cousin's yellow Volkswagen. They picked me up. While in the car, my cousin asked me, "How bad would you like to get off of pills?" I replied, "You just don't know. I will do anything to get off of pain pills." He then said, "Here, try this." I did it. The first time I tried it, I didn't feel anything. I did it again, and all of a sudden everything got so bright. It was a feeling I couldn't describe, and I loved it. That was the beginning of my crack addiction. I wanted it all the time. I did not care to sleep or eat. We would ride around all the time, thinking of lies to tell people so that we could get enough money to buy drugs.

I was the one that everyone was supposed to look up to, sort of like the rock of the family. Instead, I was the total opposite. I did everything wrong and made all the wrong moves. I blamed everyone else for my actions. I was supposed to pray to God and believe in Him to fix my problems. Instead, I decided to take His job. I often heard people say that drugs were a mind thing, and that you could quit if you really wanted to. There are case studies confirming that, but I think it depends on the strength of the person. I can remember my daughters crying for me not to leave. I was getting dressed to go to the crack house. I couldn't consider their tears or their pain at that point because drugs had messed me up so badly and so fast. When my kids would look at me, they knew who I was, but no longer viewed me as their mother. I put them in that situation. They were in need of a mother so badly. My absence caused that responsibility to fall back on my mother, even though it was not her job.

One day I came home after being gone all day, when my mother told me to get my shit and get out of her house. I said, "Okay." I didn't have anywhere to go. I figured I'd pack up my daughters, grab some bags, and all of the food I had purchased for her home. That's when things got ugly. My mother called my brother to come and put me out of her house. Once he arrived, he grabbed me and threw me out the house. I fell on the concrete and hurt my arm. I ran to my grandmother's house down the road from us. I called the police. I was sitting outside waiting for them to come to my rescue. I told the police what happened, hoping they would side with me. After speaking with my mother, they walked out of my mom's house and they came and put handcuffs on me. They took me to jail. I stayed there for three weeks. I cried and prayed the whole time. One day while still in jail, this man came to see me. He told me that if I did not sign the papers he had given to my mother for the rights to adopt my girls, that they would be in the state's custody. It was then that I felt my heart fill up with hate.

Fresh out of jail, I had a letter waiting for me from the state. It basically said that I have to prove I'm capable of raising my own daughters and that I have somewhere for them to live. They allowed me three days to straighten all of this out. Out of panic, I ran as far away as I could. The first place I stopped was the trap house. That's when I truly began to smoke crack all day, every day. When the money ran out, I would turn tricks to get more. Every time my girls would fall on my heart, I would smoke more and more crack. I did not want to remember anything. I would wear the same clothes for weeks at a time. I was turning tricks with white men, black men, and mexican men. It didn't matter to me as long as they had money with them. I eventually realized my mother was just trying to help me. She was hoping I would get off of drugs and use the letter from the state as a wakeup call. However, it only pushed me further away. Smoking dope made me numb. I could not feel the pain from my current situation. Two and a half weeks had gone by and I was still chasing that demon. For some reason I could not stop, nor did I want to.

I was at a clubhouse across town having a good time, when all of a sudden a man that I was involved with drove up and kicked me in my ass. Once I got up off the ground, I hit him with my shoe. I busted his head and in return he knocked me out cold. When I came to, I was in the hospital. My mother and my aunt were standing over me crying. I asked them where I was and they said that I was in the hospital. When the doctor discharged me, I went home with my mom. For some reason, I did not stay. I let the devil rise up in me again. I went chasing those demons. I didn't feel loved. I felt like I was floating all the time. I went back to the trap house. I began to smoke and trick and trick and smoke.

I was so high one day that I got into a car with a guy who told me that he was going to his hometown of Independence to get all the dope that we could smoke. He sold me to another man once we arrived there. I left with this guy who treated me okay. We stayed gone for a while. Once we got back, the original guy was still there waiting for me. When I got back into his car he asked me if I had something for him. I replied, "Hell no. What do you mean?" He hit me in my mouth with a gun and busted my lips. He then drove me down a dark road. After he had his way with me, he planned to kill me. No one would ever find me. He was driving about 60 to 70 miles per hour. I was undressed because he made me get out of all my clothes. I jumped out of the car. All of a sudden my body rolled down a hill. I ended up in a ditch full of water. I thanked God I didn't die. I heard his brakes squealing on the road. I jumped up and I ran through the woods as fast as I could. I was screaming until a man and his wife came outside with a gun, asking who goes there. I begged, "Please don't shoot! Please don't shoot!" All I remembered was me explaining that a man was trying to kill me. The couple let me in their house. I was still naked. I began to say my mother's phone number over and over again. Eventually, I passed out. When I came to, my mother and my sister informed me that I was

hurt pretty badly. On the bright side, I couldn't believe Jesus had chosen to spare my life again. I was released from the hospital. I went home to spend the night with my sister and her husband. The hospital would not give me anything for pain
because I was full of crack and alcohol. They instructed me to take Tylenol, but my brother-in-law gave me a pain pill to help me out.

I went back to the streets, sleeping in abandoned houses and trucks. I would wake up so hungry because I had not eaten for days. I would grab or steal a bag of chips and a cold drink from the corner stores. I was living in a bad dream and I did not want my family to see me that way. I smelled like a hog pen. I told myself that if I can get one more trick to give me about $100, I can get me a hotel room and some clothes from the dollar store. I needed to take a good bath and put some decent clothes on. I would then look good enough to go home to my family. I was tired and depressed. As I walked up and down the street, a van pulled up next to me and asked me if I needed a ride somewhere. I replied, "Yes." When I got in the van there were two white guys sitting in the

back that I did not see at first. I was very scared, but I did not let them see it. They asked how much money I wanted to do all three of them. I told them $100 for all three of them and they agreed. They drove me to a remote location. I heard them asking who would go first. One of the
men said that he would go first. He hurt me so badly, but I was afraid to say anything. Once he finished, the next one came and then the next one. I just layed there bleeding and very tired. While getting dressed, I heard one of them say, "Let's kill her." I was so afraid. I began to shake very badly and I could not stop.

All of a sudden I heard one of them say, "She did not give us any trouble. Let's take her back." They put me back in the van after I pleaded with them not to kill me. I convinced them that I wouldn't tell anyone. They drove me back to where they picked me up from. I was glad to still be alive. Two days later, they picked up a friend of mine from the same location. She was also a drug user. I warned her about the van but I guess she went for it anyway. They ended up killing her. I had beaten death again, but my friend's death made me angry. I began to talk to God while walking the backstreets. I would cry, sing, and pray very loudly, begging God for my deliverance. I asked God to remove the demon that was right on my back. I told Him I could not do this by myself and that I needed His help. I needed His love, grace and mercy. I said, "I know you did not bring me this far to leave me, God." He kept sparing my life for some reason. I could not understand why He was sparing a sinner like myself. My problem was that I knew how to treat people, I just did not know how to treat myself. One day on those same backstreets, I fell down to my knees and I cried out to God to please remove the demons that had cursed my life. I desperately needed help. All my daughters ever wanted was for me to get myself together. I had already gone through eight rehab stays. I always knew that if I kept my faith in God, the devil would flee.

This one day was a very cold day, but I was still walking the streets. I can remember this one particular day in December because it was a few days before my birthday. Hungry and very tired, some friends and I came up with enough money to buy some drugs for the day. We walked all the way to this man's house to buy some drugs. Everyone said he had the best dope. Once we made it to his house, he opened the door. It was like love at first sight for us two. I was looking at my soon-to-be husband. We must have talked all night long. I met a man that made me feel like my life was worth living. He made me feel like I had a chance to start life over with my daughters and be happy again. He was the opposite of the men I had dealt with in my past. He made me feel like I was on top of the world. He did not view me as a crackhead. He treated me like I was a black queen. It was a wonderful feeling and I wanted it to last forever. It did for a while. I moved into his house about a week after I met him. He was a drug dealer and I was a smoker. I did not care to think about how this would turn out. I was in love. I was with a man that treated me like I mattered. I smoked all the drugs I wanted for free, so I thought. We lived on Mooney Avenue in Hammond. Being that my man sold drugs there, we had a lot of traffic. I felt so important living there with him. I didn't think anyone else could come along and hurt me. I found my protection and I was happy. My girls would even come over to the house to see me sometimes.

My new man had done a background check on me and found out that my family had a little money and prominence. He felt that he could benefit from it somewhere down the line. He made all of his friends respect me, even the people I did not know. He told me that he was a retired police officer from Ponchatoula, Louisiana and I believed him. I mean, why not? It wasn't until after I married him that I found out about the real person he was. He was very selfish, mean, and didn't own anything. I found out later that I had actually tricked with one of his close relatives, prior to knowing him. How was I to know? I kept my distance from that particular relative and we went on like nothing ever happened. As time passed, my husband got meaner and began to fight me. I was so afraid of him because I had heard stories about him hurting people that he felt had crossed him. I couldn't smoke for free anymore so I had to go back to the streets while we were still together. He made me sell my body for crack, and he still would not let me go. I tried running away but he would find me and make me come back home. I was so afraid of him that I let him control my life.

My husband did not smoke but he drank a lot. One night he got very drunk and I got very high from smoking crack. We had fallen asleep, when someone threw a firebomb on our house. The house started to blaze while we were still in the bed. We almost lost our lives. Everything burned down. God had spared my life once again. We moved a lot after that. We left Hammond, Louisiana and moved to Florida. We then came back to Greensburg, Louisiana where he was originally from. After a year or so, my husband was diagnosed with cancer. He began treatment and I became his caretaker. After he got well, he began to be mean to me again. One night he went out somewhere. The next morning the police picked him up stating he was wanted for murder. He remained in police custody for 7 months. Unfortunately, the cancer had come back and he did not live to see the trial date. Needless to say, that was the end of my marriage and a continuance of my addiction.

My drug use forced my mother to have to give my daughters the extra love and time that I was unable to give to them for most of their lives. One day, I decided I was going to exercise my own power and authority over my life. The first change that I noticed was mental clarity. I knew that was one of the main keys to overcoming my addiction. My memory and my feelings began to come back, slowly. I was learning how to love again. I was out there in those streets doing God-knows-what. I had become so tired. I had nowhere else to turn, so eventually, I resorted back to God. I began to pray the kind of prayer that you would pray when you needed God to forgive you for all of your sins. By asking God for forgiveness, doors began to open that I could not seem to open on my own. I began to realize that my family had never given up on me. They had people praying for me in different cities and different states. It was me who had given up on myself. My drug-induced thoughts had me believing that no one cared about me. I was blaming myself for something that happened to me when I was younger, that I had no control over. I had to get out of that paralyzing state of mind. I've always asked myself why I couldn't stop doing drugs. You cannot start the future without completing the past. It took some of the things that I went through to mold me into who I needed to be. Those prayers from my family stopped me from totally sinking. By reading His words and seeking the knowledge to understand His words, I learned that God is indeed real. The Bible says to seek Ye first the kingdom of God and His righteousness, and all things will be added unto you. I believe that.

Today, I am 57 years old, but I've lost 32 years of my life to the world. I know that time has come and gone, but I still reflect on how I missed out on things like my girls growing into early adulthood. I hardly have any memories of their childhood, but because of God's grace and mercy, He has allowed me to be a part of my grandchildren's lives. My grandchildren love me just as hard as I love them. Nowadays, I wake up most mornings feeling a little bit better than the day before. It feels as though God woke me from a 30 year nightmare. I thank Him for blowing his breath on me, giving me another chance to appreciate the beauty of life. When I was using drugs, I could not see, nor did I care to see the world, or the beautiful people in it. All I cared about was obtaining more money to get high. Because of His love and mercy, I'm clean and sober today. Now, I can appreciate all the beautiful things in this world and how to love His people. It brings tears to my eyes. When I would leave my girls at home for my mother to babysit, I was thinking I was only going to be gone about 3 to 4 days. In reality, it was 3 to 4 years. I realized that when you let Satan take over your mind and body, he also messes with your years. He'll have you thinking it was only days that passed. I have surrendered totally to God. My girls are now 37 & 38 years old. Where has the time gone? As much as I love God, I can't believe I stopped praying and let those drugs consume me the way that I did.

Thankfully, God has broken those chains that had me bound for so long. I think the hardest question had to be how could I be away from my daughters for that amount of time? I had forgotten how it felt to give my girls a bath at night and tell them good morning, with breakfast waiting on the table. I missed out on so many trips to the park to watch them play together. My girls are now grown, with their own families, but I still have time left to be a mother and a grandmother. I can now fill that empty space that is inside of me. I now make time to speak to my sister and brothers as often as I can. There was a point in my life when I didn't care if I spoke to any of them.

Now I make it a priority to call and ask each of them how they are doing.

While walking back home one day, a truck was coming down the road. The truck approached me. I knew the guy driving the truck, but I could not remember his name. He proceeded to tell me how good I looked to him. I suggested that we go have drinks one evening. He said, "Okay. How about tonight?" I then had an epiphany. I replied, "I don't even drink anymore. Let's start over." I proceeded to ask if he and his family enjoyed the holidays that had just passed. I also informed him that my mother and family have bible study every Saturday at her home. "You can sit in if you want to. You and your family." I extended an offer. He replied, "Okay. That sounds nice. I will talk to you about it later." He then drove off. It hit me that he was not interested in the new Debbie. He wanted the old Debbie. He never even took my number to call, to confirm his disinterest in the changed version of me.

In no way am I saying I'm perfect now, but my life has become less difficult by praying and reading His words. Now, I'm able to accept the things I cannot change. I had to go through so much to become who I'm destined to be. Sometimes you have to go through the desert to get to a little rose that has been sitting in the middle of it the whole time, just waiting to be discovered and watered. My journey has been hard, but worth it. I have the scars to prove it. I may not be where I want to be, but I'm definitely not where I used to be. God is still holding my hand.

About the Authors

As of September 2020, Debra and her two daughters, April and Krystal, are rebuilding their family piece by piece. Debra is enjoying quarantining with her grandchildren during the pandemic. She splits her time and love evenly amongst them. April is an active member in the community, participating in several organizations to promote growth for black-owned businesses. She also enjoys spending time with her children and her fiance. Krystal resides in Independence, Louisiana with her children. Between a demanding career and making sure that her kids are academically inclined, Krystal stays busy. To follow their progress, they can all be reached on social media under their respective names.

www.ingramcontent.com/pod-product-compliance
Lightning Source LLC
Chambersburg PA
CBHW062201100526
44589CB00014B/1905